Cornerstones of Freedom

The Story of

THE BLACK HAWK WAR

By Jim Hargrove

Illustrated by Ralph Canaday

 CHILDRENS PRESS ®

CHICAGO

Library of Congress Cataloging-in-Publication Data

Hargrove, Jim.
   The story of the Black Hawk War.

   (Cornerstones of freedom)
   Summary: Relates the events, as recalled by the
Sauk Indian chief, Black Hawk, that led to the last
great Indian uprising east of the Mississippi River in
1832.
   1.   Black Hawk War, 1832—Juvenile literature.
2.   Black Hawk, Sauk chief, 1767-1838—Juvenile
literature.   3.   Sauk Indians—Juvenile literature.
[1.   Black Hawk War, 1832-   .   2.   Black Hawk,
Sauk chief, 1767-1838.   3.   Sauk Indians.   4.   Indians
of North America]   I. Title.   II.   Series.
E83.83.H34   1986   973.5′6   86-955
ISBN 0-516-04696-9

"Why did the Great Spirit ever send the whites to this island, to drive us from our homes, and introduce among us poisonous liquors, disease and death? They should have remained on the island where the Great Spirit first placed them."

These words were spoken by the Sauk Indian warrior Black Hawk. In 1832 he led the last great Indian uprising east of the Mississippi River. But as wars go, the Black Hawk affair was almost insignificant. Fewer than seventy white soldiers and settlers were killed, although far more Indians died. On the final day of the short war, as many as two hundred Indians, including many women and children, were slaughtered, partly by mistake.

The Black Hawk War is one of the saddest stories in American history, but it is also one of the most remarkable. Among the young men who joined the army to fight against Black Hawk were two future presidents, Abraham Lincoln and Zachary Taylor. Another volunteer was Jefferson Davis, the man who would become president of the Confederacy during the Civil War. Sons of Alexander Hamilton and Daniel Boone also joined the army.

Men like Lincoln and Taylor would rise to national importance despite their participation in the shameful war. But the old Indian warrior Black Hawk was ruined by the rebellion he began. Nevertheless, almost unique among great Indian leaders, Black Hawk managed to publish an autobiography, his life story in book form.

With a few additions and corrections, this is Black Hawk's story.

Since the time Black Hawk was born in 1767, the Sauk Indians and their close friends the Fox had lived along the Rock River near the Mississippi in northwestern Illinois. Except when they were warring with other groups of Indians, the Sauk would travel south down the Mississippi each year to a village named Saint Louis.

In Saint Louis, Black Hawk and his friends would visit a man Black Hawk called his "Spanish father," actually a Spanish colonial official. After a long absence because of a fight with other Indian tribes over hunting grounds, the Sauk Indians traveled once again to Saint Louis and found their Spanish friends happy to see them again.

"After painting and dressing," Black Hawk said in his book, "we called to see our Spanish father and were well received. He gave us a variety of presents, and plenty of provisions. We danced through the town as usual, and its inhabitants all seemed to be well pleased. They appeared to us like brothers— and always gave us good advice."

Black Hawk and the Sauk Indians would make but one more friendly visit to Saint Louis, this time in 1804. But as soon as the travelers arrived, they could see that much had changed. Black Hawk noticed that all the Spanish soldiers and traders looked unhappy.

"I inquired the cause," Black Hawk said, "and was informed that the Americans were coming to take possession of the town and country—and that we should then lose our Spanish father. This news made myself and band sad—because we had always heard bad accounts of the Americans from Indians who had lived near them—and we were sorry to lose our Spanish father, who had always treated us with great friendship."

The event that had taken place was the Louisiana Purchase. On March 9, 1804, an American captain had come to Saint Louis to take control of a huge tract of land west of the Mississippi. Spain had ceded this land to France a few years earlier, and the United States had purchased it from France. The Louisiana Purchase nearly doubled the size of the U.S. As Black Hawk would learn much later, this meant trouble for the Sauk Indians.

Black Hawk returned to his village on the Rock

River. Soon a boat carrying a small group of
American soldiers led by Lieutenant Zebulon Pike
sailed into the Sauk village. It was Pike who, two
years later, would discover the famous mountain
called Pike's Peak while exploring the western lands
of the Louisiana Purchase.

Pike gave presents to the Indians and made a
speech. The new American fathers, he insisted,
would treat the Sauk well. He also presented the
Indians with an American flag. It would be best,
Pike added, to lower the British flag that was
hoisted on a pole in the village. "This we declined,"
Black Hawk said in his autobiography, "as we
wished to have two Fathers!"

A few months later, a series of events occurred which Black Hawk later said were the source of all the troubles leading to the Black Hawk War. A Sauk Indian, involved in a fight with some American settlers, had killed three of them. Knowing this could lead to serious problems, the Sauk Indians selected four braves to travel to Saint Louis to meet with the new American fathers. The Indians were gone from the village for some time.

When they returned, they were wearing fine new coats and had shiny medals hanging on their chests. The story they reported about their visit, however, was disturbing. The Indian involved in the killings had been imprisoned in Saint Louis. While the four Sauk visitors were still trying to talk officials into freeing him, the Indian had either escaped or been released, and was shot dead by American soldiers.

It was later proven that the white settlers the Indian had killed had actually attacked the Indian first. He had killed in self-defense. President Thomas Jefferson sent a letter pardoning the Indian to Saint Louis, but it arrived too late.

There was even worse news of the visit to Saint Louis. When the Sauk visitors asked their new American father, whose name was William Henry

Harrison, to release the Sauk prisoner, Harrison seemed to change the subject. The white settlers, he explained, needed more land. After some discussion, the Indians signed a paper giving the whites some land west of the Mississippi River and a small amount, they thought, east of the river.

The Americans apparently did not mention that the treaty gave the U.S. government all Sauk and Fox land, including the Indians' own villages. But the four Sauk visitors could remember little of what happened in Saint Louis. The Americans had given them much whiskey during their visit. "They had been drunk the greater part of the time they were in St. Louis," Black Hawk said.

Not until 1818 did Black Hawk discover that the four Indians, who had no authority to speak for the entire Sauk tribe, had signed a treaty giving away all the land of the Sauk people in return for a payment of $1,000 per year by the U.S. government. Black Hawk refused to accept any more payments after that year.

In the meantime, much had happened between the Sauk and the American people. For years British soldiers, operating from Canada, had encouraged Indians to resist the westward movement of American settlers. Then the U.S. Congress declared war on Great Britain on June 8, 1812. While battles raged in Canada, along the eastern seacoast, and around the Gulf of Mexico, many Indians, including the Sauk, became involved in skirmishes along the frontier, fighting on the British side.

With the help of British soldiers, the Sauk and other Indian tribes managed to drive the Americans out of northwestern Illinois and Wisconsin. Despite repeated attempts to regain the territory, the American troops were defeated.

But the greatest battles of the War of 1812 were fought elsewhere, and in those battles the British did not fare so well. The British lost the war and

were forced to abandon the Indians who had been their allies. American military governors demanded that many Indian tribes sign peace treaties with the American government.

One by one, Indian tribes along the frontier began signing treaties. In September 1815, Black Hawk and the Sauk Indians were supposed to travel to a small settlement near where the Mississippi and Missouri rivers met, to sign a peace agreement. They did not complete the journey because, according to Black Hawk, one of their chiefs became ill.

Then Black Hawk learned that American troops would be sent to fight the Sauk if the Indians did not soon sign the agreement. So the following year, he and other Sauk Indians traveled to Saint Louis. There they were met by soldiers who were angered that they had not yet signed the treaty.

After angry words were spoken on both sides, an agreement seemed to be reached and a peace pipe was smoked. "Here, for the first time," Black Hawk reported, "I touched the goose quill to the treaty—not knowing, however, that, by that act, I consented to give away my village. Had that been explained to me, I should certainly have opposed it, and never would have signed their treaty."

The treaty that Black Hawk signed—but did not understand—reaffirmed the conditions of the treaty of 1804, which gave all Sauk and Fox land to the American government. Although it would soon be ignored by white settlers, the treaty of 1804 clearly gave the Sauk Indians the right to live and hunt on the land as long as it was owned by the U.S. government. The treaty made no mention of what would happen to the Indians if American settlers came to own the land. It was a cruel trick, and probably no oversight.

"What do we know of the manner of the laws and customs of the white people?" Black Hawk asked. "They might buy our bodies for dissection, and we would touch the goose quill to confirm it, without knowing what we were doing."

The years passed, and for a time no disastrous

consequences came of the two treaties the Sauk had signed. More white settlers came to the land of the Rock River, but hunts and harvests were good, and all seemed to live in peace. But by the summer of 1829, everything began to change.

That year, a trader named George Davenport came to live at the settlement of Rock Island, not far from the Sauk village. With Davenport was the U.S. government agent in charge of the Sauk Indians. The two began insisting that the Sauk would have to leave their village. For the first time, Black Hawk learned that the treaties of 1804 and 1816 did not even give the Sauk the right to live on the land that was once theirs. Keokuk, an important Sauk chief, already had been persuaded to move to Iowa on the west side of the Mississippi.

Black Hawk was shocked, and urged the other Sauk Indians not to move. He asked Keokuk to travel to Saint Louis to talk with the American father there. Keokuk would ask for permission to travel to Washington, D.C., and talk with the great father. With that plan made, Black Hawk and the other Sauk made ready to leave their village, as they did each winter, to travel south to hunt. His own words describe what happened next.

"During the winter, I received information that three families of whites had arrived at our village, and destroyed some of our lodges, and were making fences and dividing our cornfields for their own use—and were quarreling among themselves about their lines, in the division! I immediately started for Rock River, a distance of ten days' travel, and on my arrival found the report to be true. I went to my lodge, and found a family occupying it."

Black Hawk could speak little English, and could not tell the settlers to go away. He spoke to several Indian agents and interpreters, but most advised him to move across the Mississippi with Keokuk. Eventually, he returned to the hunting grounds to the south.

When the Indians returned to their village in the spring of 1830, they found that more white settlers had moved onto their land. Many of their lodges had been burned or destroyed. The Americans had built fences enclosing most of the seven hundred acres of Sauk cornfields. One of Black Hawk's friends found an island in the Rock River with a plot of ground to plant corn in, but soon a white settler plowed it up and replanted it with his own corn.

For the settlers, guns, traps, and horses were scarce. But there seemed to be plenty of whiskey, which they offered to any Sauk who wished to drink. Soon, many Indians were thirsty enough to trade rifles, horses, and traps for liquor. Angered over what he called the "bad medicine," Black Hawk smashed at least one settler's barrel of whiskey.

During the summer, a young Indian opened an
American's fence to let his horse pass through and
was beaten to death by two club-wielding settlers.
Several Sauk women were attacked.

Although many of the settlers complained that the
Indians were trespassing on their property, actually
just the opposite was true. Most of the Americans
were squatters—settlers who were living on land
they had not yet purchased. Even by the harsh
terms of the treaty of 1804, the Sauk Indians still
had the right to live on most of the land that had
been their village.

Black Hawk complained to two Americans he called chiefs, a former Illinois governor and a judge. "I told them that the white people had already entered our village," he said, "burnt our lodges, destroyed our fences, ploughed up our corn, and beat our people; that they had brought whiskey into our country, made our people drunk, and taken from them their horses, guns, and traps; and that I had borne all this injury, without suffering any of my braves to raise a hand against the whites."

In the fall, he learned that parts of his village lands were now being purchased from the government. They were bought by George Davenport, the trader who had first told the Sauk to leave their village. The news infuriated Black Hawk, but still he did not resort to violence.

News came from the Sauk Indians who had followed Keokuk to Iowa, and it wasn't good. The soil west of the Mississippi had never been broken by a plow. Keokuk's followers had not been able to plow up enough ground to plant sufficient corn for the winter. Hunting there was poor as well.

Black Hawk's followers faced an equally grim future. Traveling south to the Sauk's winter hunting grounds, the tribe now no longer carried enough rifles and traps to allow a good hunt. And most of the corn planted the previous spring had been destroyed by the Americans.

When the Sauk returned to their village in early spring, the old chief, now more than sixty years old, made a desperate offer to save his people. They would leave their village forever, Black Hawk said, if the government would make a payment of $6,000. With this the Indians could buy food, traps, and rifles, now desperately needed for the hunt.

The answer to Black Hawk's request was provided by General Edmund P. Gaines, who sailed down the Rock River on a steamboat with seven hundred soldiers. On June 4, 1831, General Gaines and Black Hawk met face-to-face.

"I came here," the general said, "neither to beg nor hire you to leave your village. My business is to remove you, peaceably if I can, but forcibly if I must! I will now give you two days to remove in— and if you do not cross the Mississippi within that time, I will adopt measures to force you away!"

The meeting broke up in anger when Black Hawk said that he would never leave his village. He knew that he was in a difficult position. About a third of his followers had fled across the Mississippi at the

first sight of Gaines's soldiers. Although Black
Hawk might have been able to raise about five
hundred warriors, they were poorly fed and even
more poorly armed. Had he been able to raise a
greater resistance, he would almost certainly have
gone to war immediately.

Instead, he told his followers to return to their
lodges and await their deaths! And he stalled for
time by asking to be allowed to remain in the village
until fall, when he promised to leave for the western
land. General Gaines refused the request.

The general, however, was not ready for all-out
war. The two-day deadline passed without event.
For more than a month, the American army and the
Sauk warriors made ready for battle, but there was
no actual fighting.

On July 28, an even larger army of American soldiers—this time, mounted volunteers organized by the governor of Illinois—appeared on the south bank of the Rock River. At the sight of this second army, the Sauk Indians realized that their situation was hopeless. They fled across the Mississippi.

A few days later, Black Hawk crossed the wide river again, this time carrying the white flag of surrender. He met once more with Gaines, and signed another paper. In return, Black Hawk was promised enough corn to keep his people from starving.

The American squatters at the old Sauk village refused to honor the terms of the new agreement. The Indians spent a miserable winter on the west bank of the Mississippi. The Americans gave the Indians so little corn that, as Black Hawk noted, the Sauk were forced "to steal corn from their own fields." Gunfire was exchanged a number of times during the winter corn raids.

Black Hawk was through with words and paper promises. During the horrible winter, he tried to persuade other Indian tribes, particularly the Potawatomi, Winnebago, Sioux, and Kickapoo, to join him in the battle to rid the Mississippi valley of the hated Americans. But by spring, only his good friends the Fox Indians agreed to join the battle.

Claiming that they were moving in peace, but fully armed, a band of more than six hundred Sauk and Fox warriors under Black Hawk's leadership crossed the Mississippi into Illinois on April 5, 1832. Word quickly reached Washington that Indians were on the warpath in the northern Mississippi valley. A large group of militia and regular soldiers was organized under Brigadier General Henry Atkinson, with Colonel Zachary Taylor second in command.

"My party having all come in and got ready,"
Black Hawk said, "we commenced our march up the
Mississippi, our women and children in canoes,
carrying such provisions as we had." Many of the
Americans living along the Mississippi frontier
quickly fled east. A number found refuge in a rough
frontier town called Chicago.

Atkinson and his army traveled up the Mississippi
in steamboats, ahead of the Indians who were also
traveling north. Black Hawk finally reached the
Rock River, where he would turn east to reach his
village. There he fully expected the Americans to be
waiting in ambush. "We commenced beating our
drums and singing," Black Hawk said, "to show the
Americans that we were not afraid."

But Atkinson's army did not attack. Instead, messengers were sent up the Rock River demanding that Black Hawk return to the land west of the Mississippi. The old warrior refused.

With Atkinson's huge army in pursuit, Black Hawk realized that his situation was hopeless. He decided to give up and return to the west side of the Mississippi. He appointed three braves to carry the white flag of surrender to the American army, and sent five others to watch the truce makers from a distance.

When the Indians carrying word of the surrender reached an advance force of 270 soldiers under the command of Major Isaiah Stillman, the peace flag was ignored. The three braves carrying the white flag were captured, and two of the Indians sent to watch the event were killed. The war that should have ended at this point now moved into full swing.

Enraged at the treatment of his messengers, Black Hawk attacked Stillman's troops with fifty or sixty of his braves. To his astonishment, the American soldiers fled. "I expected to see them fight as the Americans did with the British during the last war," Black Hawk said, "but they had no such braves among them."

After the American defeat in the battle that became known as "Stillman's Run," the entire army under General Atkinson returned to its base in Ottawa, Illinois, where many of the soldiers were released from duty. Encouraged by Black Hawk's astonishing victory, a group of Winnebago Indians decided to join him, and soon others did as well.

An American general named Winfield Scott tried to organize another army to attack the Indians, but his men were attacked—by disease. A severe cholera epidemic broke out in Scott's camp and his army became too weak to move.

Finally, in June of 1832, General Atkinson reorganized the army that would put a bloody end to Black Hawk's rebellion. This huge army included more than a thousand volunteer militia, in addition to regular soldiers. In the ranks were Colonel Zachary Taylor, Captain Abraham Lincoln, and Lieutenant Jefferson Davis.

Atkinson's army headed north, but had difficulty locating the starving band of Indians, who had retreated into Wisconsin. Many of the temporary volunteers had to be released. Abraham Lincoln was mustered out of service in mid-July. He took no part in the slaughter that soon followed.

With the huge army advancing rapidly from the south, Black Hawk knew that his warriors, traveling with women and children, had no chance to win. Ravaging the frontier settlements as they moved through southern Wisconsin, the Indians decided to make a race for the Mississippi. From there they might be able to escape to the west.

Along the Wisconsin River, a large party of American soldiers caught up with the Indians, who were trying to move their women and children to an island in the river for protection. In the Battle of Wisconsin Heights that followed, Black Hawk said that only six of his men were killed. Other Sauk chiefs said that more men died from wounds while trying to reach the Mississippi. A Sauk woman reported that sixty-eight Indians were killed.

The Indians made a desperate crossing of the Wisconsin River to flee from the attacking army. Some sailed downstream toward the Mississippi in canoes. Years later, Jefferson Davis said that he saw mothers putting their babies on pieces of bark to float them across the wide river.

On August 1, 1832, the exhausted and starving survivors of Black Hawk's band reached the Mississippi, near where it is joined by the Bad Axe

River in western Wisconsin. Even though the Sioux Indians—no friends of the Sauk—lived on the other side, Black Hawk knew he had to try to cross.

Advancing rapidly from the east was Atkinson's army of sixteen hundred heavily-armed men. But upon reaching the river, the Sauk discovered that it was patrolled by a gunship and an army.

There was nothing to do but surrender. Black Hawk raised a white flag and asked to come aboard the steamship *Warrior*. Suddenly, a Winnebago aboard the ship shouted for Black Hawk to run because the whites were going to shoot.

A number of Indians were killed in the first few minutes of the Battle of Bad Axe. Many surviving Indians managed to hide behind trees and fallen logs along the shore. But one of the saddest chapters in

American history occurred the next day. Here is how Black Hawk described it.

"Early in the morning a party of whites, being in advance of the army, came upon our people, who were attempting to cross the Mississippi. They tried to give themselves up—the whites paid no attention to their entreaties—but commenced slaughtering them! In a little while the whole army arrived. Our braves, but few in number, finding that the enemy paid no regard to age or sex, and seeing that they were murdering helpless women and little children, determined to fight until they were killed! As many as could, commenced swimming the Mississippi, with their children on their backs. A number of them were drowned, and some shot, before they could reach the opposite shore."

Between 150 and 200 Indian men, women, and children were killed in the Battle of Bad Axe. Six American soldiers died. According to a Sauk chief, about 200 Indians made it across the river, where many were slaughtered by the Sioux.

Somehow, old chief Black Hawk managed to escape the slaughter. He and a small band of Indians had headed north the evening before, instead of crossing the river. Black Hawk had given each of his followers the right to decide whether to follow him or try to cross the Mississippi.

Black Hawk surrendered to American authorities and was imprisoned and forced to wear a ball and chain. Some months later, he was taken to Washington to meet President Andrew Jackson. After more months of imprisonment, the old warrior was taken on a tour of the great cities of the East Coast, where curious crowds greeted him with something not unlike friendship. Black Hawk was astonished by the size of cities like Philadelphia and New York. He now knew that it would be impossible for Indians to stop the westward movement of the whites.

Black Hawk finally moved to the land west of the Mississippi, but even that would be lost in his

lifetime. In 1836 and 1837, Keokuk, now the clear leader of the Sauk and Fox, was forced to sell the land to pay off debts. In 1838, when he was more than seventy years old, Black Hawk and his family moved to land along the Des Moines River.

At the conclusion of the Black Hawk War in 1832, the population of Sauk and Fox Indians was somewhere around 5,000. By 1937, it was about 1,400. In 1970, about 450 Sauk and Fox Indians were living on reservations in Iowa, Kansas, and Oklahoma.

About the Author

Jim Hargrove has worked as a writer and editor for more than ten years. After serving as an editorial director for three Chicago area publishers, he began a career as an independent writer, preparing a series of books for children. He has contributed to works by nearly twenty different publishers. His Childrens Press titles are *Mark Twain: The Story of Samuel Clemens, Richard Nixon: The Thirty-Seventh President,* and *Microcomputers at Work.* With his wife and daughter, he lives in a small Illinois town near the Wisconsin border.

About the Artist

Ralph Canaday has been involved in all aspects of commercial art since graduation from the Art Institute of Chicago in 1959. He is an illustrator, designer, painter, and sculptor whose work has appeared in many national publications, texbooks, and corporate promotional material. Mr. Canaday lives in Hanover Park, Illinois, with his wife Arlene, who is also in publishing.